Franklin & Eleanor

Written and illustrated by

Cheryl Harness

DUTTON CHILDREN'S BOOKS • NEW YORK

"Happiness lies not in the mere possession of money;
it lies in the joy of achievement, in the thrill of creative effort."
—FRANKLIN DELANO ROOSEVELT, MARCH 4, 1933

AUTHOR'S NOTE

When Americans today see photos of Franklin D. Roosevelt, they see a smiling "fat cat" with a big chin and an upraised cigarette holder. Look at that smile as his fellow Americans did: against a backdrop of dark, fearful times; then what you see is jaunty encouragement. His strong voice lifted them up when he told them, in 1933, that only the fear in their hearts was worth being afraid of. In 1941, the people still turned to him, though he'd grown old and ill, to guide them through the huge nightmare of World War II. Hardly any of them knew, as they elected "FDR" to four terms in office, that every day their smiling, powerful president had to work around paralysis from the polio that had nearly killed him. Hardly any of them knew that their plain-featured, much-traveled First Lady, Eleanor Roosevelt, had survived a lonely, tragic childhood *and* a domineering mother-in-law to become a tireless worker for social justice. The story of Franklin and Eleanor is a story of overcoming.

Franklin and Eleanor were complicated people who overcame many sorrows and used their partnership and their lives, lived in the best and worst of times, to forever change the relationship between the citizens of the United States and their government. Because of this, the Roosevelts inspired strong feelings, admiring and otherwise, in Americans of their time. Because of this, theirs is a story worth telling, and the theme of that story was best expressed by Eleanor: "It's your life—but only if you make it so."

*As this book was written for no other reason than to honor
the lives of Eleanor and Franklin, it is dedicated to their memory.*
C.H.

CIP Data is available.

Published in the United States by Dutton Children's Books,
a division of Penguin Young Readers Group
345 Hudson Street, New York, New York 10014
www.penguin.com

Designed by Sara Reynolds and Richard Amari

Manufactured in China
First Edition
1 3 5 7 9 10 8 6 4 2
ISBN 0-525-47259-2

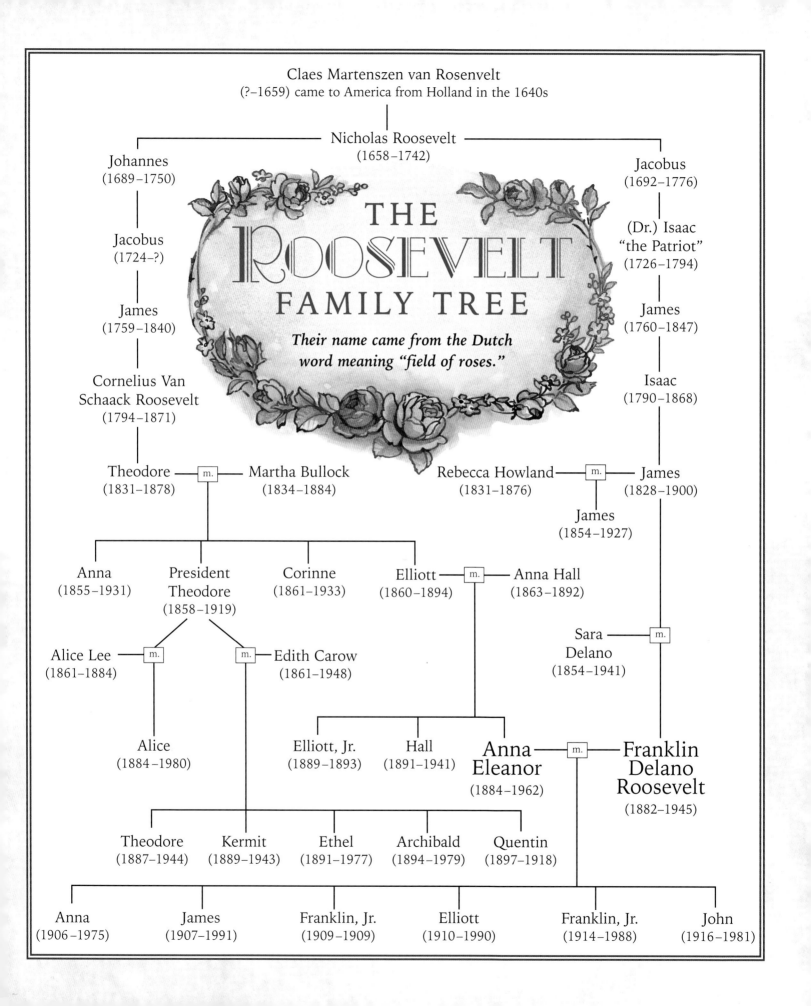

Claes Martenszen van Rosenvelt
(?–1659) came to America from Holland in the 1640s

Nicholas Roosevelt
(1658–1742)

Johannes
(1689–1750)

Jacobus
(1692–1776)

THE ROOSEVELT
FAMILY TREE

Their name came from the Dutch
word meaning "field of roses."

Jacobus
(1724–?)

(Dr.) Isaac
"the Patriot"
(1726–1794)

James
(1759–1840)

James
(1760–1847)

Cornelius Van
Schaack Roosevelt
(1794–1871)

Isaac
(1790–1868)

Theodore
(1831–1878) — m. — Martha Bullock
(1834–1884)

Rebecca Howland
(1831–1876) — m. — James
(1828–1900)

James
(1854–1927)

Anna
(1855–1931)

President
Theodore
(1858–1919)

Corinne
(1861–1933)

Elliott — m. — Anna Hall
(1860–1894)   (1863–1892)

Sara — m.
Delano
(1854–1941)

Alice Lee — m.
(1861–1884)

m. — Edith Carow
(1861–1948)

Alice
(1884–1980)

Elliott, Jr.
(1889–1893)

Hall
(1891–1941)

Anna — m. — Franklin
Eleanor   Delano
(1884–1962)   Roosevelt
(1882–1945)

Theodore
(1887–1944)

Kermit
(1889–1943)

Ethel
(1891–1977)

Archibald
(1894–1979)

Quentin
(1897–1918)

Anna
(1906–1975)

James
(1907–1991)

Franklin, Jr.
(1909–1909)

Elliott
(1910–1990)

Franklin, Jr.
(1914–1988)

John
(1916–1981)

DEEP IN THE WINTER OF 1882, in an upstairs bedroom of a big house on a high, winter-white bluff over the Hudson River, a baby was born. His parents, James and Sara, called their house "Springwood." They named their boy Franklin Delano Roosevelt.

Sara adored her little son. He called her "Mumpsy." Not until he was four would she cut his golden curls and pack them carefully away. James, also known as "Popsy," was a wealthy and important businessman who gave his son a princely life of ponies and sailboats, tutors and governesses, ocean voyages to Europe and visits to their summer house on Campobello Island near the coast of Maine.

In 1887, James and Sara took five-year-old Franklin to visit the White House. The big, red-faced president, Grover Cleveland, took the little boy's hand in his own enormous one and told him, "My little man, I am making a strange wish for you. It is that you may never be president of the United States."

On October 11, 1884, when Franklin was not quite three years old, his distant cousin was born in New York City. Her parents, Elliott and Anna, named their baby Anna Eleanor. She would go by her middle name and so be known as Eleanor Roosevelt.

When she was a little girl, Eleanor loved to watch her mother being laced into a glittering gown, getting ready for an evening out with Eleanor's father, who looked dashing with his waxed mustache and gleaming top hat. When Elliott was away from home, Eleanor would stroke her mother's brow to soothe away the fearful headaches. But beautiful Anna could not hide her disappointment in her daughter's chin, which went in, and her teeth, which stuck out. "You're so plain," Anna would say with a sigh.

The best times for Eleanor were when she and her father walked hand in hand along the streets of New York. He told her about wonderful places in the world and promised that together they would see them all someday. Eleanor loved him and the way he called her his good "Little Nell" who would grow up to be a great lady. Her mother called her "Granny"—even in front of company! But her father frequently smelled of whiskey. He left promises unkept and, more and more often, he was away from home.

When Eleanor was eight years old, her mother died of diphtheria. Several months later, scarlet fever killed her little brother Elliott, Jr. Worst of all, Eleanor's beloved father died in the summer of 1894, his dreams all drunk up. Eleanor's grim grandmother made a home for the sad-eyed girl and her three-year-old brother, Hall.

Four years later, fourteen-year-old Eleanor stood, miserable, plain, and uncertain, on the fringes of a Christmas party. She wore a babyish, too short dress picked out by her grandmother. Her cousin Alice Roosevelt, Uncle Theodore's fashionable, smart-alecky daughter, teased their distant cousin Franklin until he asked Eleanor to dance. When Eleanor sailed away to school in England a few months later, she took with her the memory of that dance. Along with the nineteenth century, perhaps her gloomy childhood was coming to an end.

In 1900, Franklin, who was a student at Harvard University, got word that his father had died of a heart gone frail. Harvard was where Uncle Theodore had gone to school. Since his Rough Rider days in the Spanish-American War, "Uncle Ted" had become the governor of New York, vice president of the United States, and hero to Franklin and the nation. Franklin, who seemed always to be trying too hard to be liked, was no hero to his classmates. He was a non-athletic boy among rough-and-tumble fellows at school and college. Franklin's mother, Sara, moved to Boston to be nearer her son. She was sure that behind his cheerful smile was a boy who needed her. Lonely Sara certainly needed him.

At her private school outside London, Eleanor had found a hero of her own: her teacher. Mademoiselle Souvestre expected much of her students, these rich men's daughters. They would speak only French, play sports, and read deeply. Eleanor began to shine in this strict world of ideals and purposeful living. She made friends and plans. She would teach and help to make the world a better place. She would be the confident, noble, happy woman of her father's dreams.

Her grandmother had another plan. Eighteen-year-old Eleanor must come home and be presented to the highest society of New York—especially to those with acceptable sons who might overlook her teeth and bookish mind and offer to marry her. This was a young lady's only proper career decision. Eleanor gave in to her grandmother, a very firm character.

A more polished and self-assured Eleanor did begin to see a very handsome and wealthy young man. He invited her to dances and football games at Harvard, where he was studying history and editing the university paper. They talked about books as they rode horses through the woods along the Hudson River. She introduced him to a world he'd never known when she took him to the settlement house where, as a volunteer, she taught exercises and dancing to immigrant children.

Eleanor delighted in the seriousness hidden behind her boyfriend's engaging smile. Young Franklin Roosevelt, in turn, was so delighted in slender, earnest Eleanor, so unlike any of the high-society girls he knew, that he asked her to marry him.

People eagerly accepted invitations to their wedding on March 17, 1905. All eyes were riveted on spectacular, bespectacled Uncle Theodore—TR, the twenty-sixth president of the United States—who gave away the bride and stole the show.

The newlyweds would live with Franklin's mother, Sara, at Springwood on the Hudson, but they also needed a city house. Sara had one built on East Sixty-fifth Street—right next door to her own. How handy! Franklin would finish his studies at Columbia University and become a lawyer. As was the custom in Eleanor's time, her main job would be being Mrs. Roosevelt, aristocratic bride.

Sara would advise the poor motherless girl on everything Franklin's wife should know and, when the babies came along, help her raise Franklin's children. Anna was born in 1906; then came James; Franklin, Jr., was born—and died—in 1909; then Elliott and another little Franklin. By the time baby John was born in 1916, war had taken over Europe, and Sara had taken over shy, uncertain Eleanor.

When America entered World War I in 1917, Franklin tried to become a sailor, but he was needed in Washington, D.C. At the time he was, as TR had been, the assistant secretary of the Navy. In spite of Sara's objections and Eleanor's reluctance at being a politician's wife, Franklin was chasing a dream. He hoped to become America's next President Roosevelt.

In the months after the deadly Great War came to an end, Uncle TR died, and Franklin stepped into the hot national spotlight for the first time as the Democratic vice presidential candidate. Although he and his running mate lost the election of 1920, Franklin felt certain that he had a part to play in the drama of American politics.

The following summer, he and Eleanor took their children to visit Campobello Island. It was there that Franklin got sick. Suddenly, curiously, and painfully sick.

A terrifying virus called polio nearly killed thirty-nine-year-old Franklin Roosevelt. Then it stole his ability to walk and—in spite of his determination, doctors, hurtful exercises, and treatments—never gave it back. He focused all of the power of his mind as he commanded, willed even one useless toe to move. It was no use.

All of the Roosevelts tried their best to mask their fear, sadness, anger, and pain. Why had this happened? Would Franklin be an invalid, a prisoner in a sickroom? The idea of a fire especially frightened him—what if he couldn't escape? Franklin puffed, sweated, and worked to strengthen the muscles in his arms and upper body until one day he was able to show his wife how he could drag his paralyzed legs across the floor to safety. Eleanor couldn't hold back her tears.

Franklin faced another question: Would polio take away his career in politics? Not if Louis Howe could help it. When Franklin was a young senator in New York's capital, he had befriended this tough-talking reporter. Through a cloud of his own cigarette smoke, Mr. Howe could always sniff which way the political winds were blowing. He still believed that Franklin D. Roosevelt had a bright future, and he had a plan. While Franklin worked on getting better, Eleanor must not let him be forgotten. By golly, women had won the right to vote in 1920! There was political work to be done, and Eleanor must help do it.

Sara couldn't stand smelly, messy Mr. Howe. Surely Franklin must come home to Springwood, where his mother would look after him. He could tend his stamp and model-ship collections. Politics? Eleanor out making speeches? Certainly not—the very idea!

Could Franklin and Eleanor see themselves shut away from the world of action, forever under Sara's wing? Certainly not! Out on his sailboat, at his desk, while doing his exercises, and during his struggle to walk on crutches, Franklin had a victory to win over his body and his mind.

Eleanor began learning how government worked and, with Mr. Howe's coaching, how to make speeches. She discovered her talents for writing, for organizing meetings and committees, and for coming up with strategies to win better lives for women, children, black people, and low-wage workers. As people responded to her kindness and hard work, Eleanor became a well-known Democrat in her own right.

As her confidence grew, Eleanor began teaching part-time at a girls' school in New York City. To provide jobs for her neighbors, she and some of her newfound friends started a furniture company near the big Roosevelt house in Hyde Park. She and Franklin talked about politics, the progress each was making, and the house that he was designing for his wife. A cottage of Eleanor's very own, it would be built a couple of miles from Sara's mansion. Franklin and Eleanor were becoming the strong characters they would be for the rest of their lives.

In 1924, Franklin discovered that he seemed to feel better in the balmy mineral water at an old resort in Warm Springs, Georgia. Over the following years he created a second home for himself there and a place where he and other polio sufferers could build their health. He designed a car that could be driven with hand controls and got to know his neighbors, poor folks just getting by. His "trial by fire," as Eleanor called his illness, taught the young prince of Springwood humility and an understanding of what it was like to be help-

less. Franklin brought this knowledge with him when he was ready to reenter politics.

On June 28, 1928, in Houston, Texas, he was scheduled to speak to a national convention of his party. Here was his chance to be seen as a strong person who had come back from the edge of death. He knew that Americans would not vote for a crippled man to lead them. He worked hard on a method that would make thousands of people think he was walking—without crutches—across the stage. Could he do it?

His right hand gripped his cane. His left hand gripped the strong arm of his son, twenty-year-old James. Slowly Franklin shifted his weight from one heavy, steel-braced leg to the other until he gripped the podium. Sweat poured down his face as he beamed an easy, triumphant smile on the cheering crowd.

Less than five months later, Franklin was elected governor of New York. He was re-elected by a landslide two years later, in the fall of 1930. By then, something awful had happened to the country, and no one knew how to fix it.

There had been hard times in America before—in 1837, 1893, 1907—when the economy sputtered. But the Great Depression that began on October 29, 1929, was the worst ever, and it was spreading around the world. The values of business stocks fell fast and hard, taking people's savings down with them. Frightened people bought as little as possible. No buying and selling meant no manufacturing and no hiring. Farmers, miners, and factory workers who had never had much of anything now were losing everything. Families who couldn't pay their bills were losing their homes and farms. They hit the road, looking for any kind of work. They lined up at soup kitchens, slept in their cars, or camped in "hobo jungles." Gloomy President Herbert Hoover figured that what went down would sooner or later go up, and besides, the government had no business getting too involved in business— or charity, for that matter.

Meanwhile, people were noticing what cheerful Governor Roosevelt of New York had been doing. He got farmers a break on their taxes. He created systems that helped the elderly and the jobless. As it was hard for him to travel, Franklin asked Eleanor to be his "eyes and ears" in the state hospitals and prisons. She returned with plenty of reports and advice. Folks began to see the Roosevelts as people who were trying hard to make their lives better. The couple's relentless work led Franklin to the Democratic convention of 1932, this time as a presidential candidate. He looked out on a crowd of politicians puffing cigars and sweltering in their seersucker suits. "I pledge you, I pledge myself," he told them, "to a new deal for the American people."

Later that month, an army of war veterans
and their families marched to Washington.
Congress had promised to pay them each a
bonus—in 1945. But these hungry folks
needed money now! They camped near the
White House and, having nowhere to go,
wouldn't leave, even after they were denied
their money. President Hoover sent soldiers
to run them off with tear gas and bayonets.

The country was falling apart. Could a new
president put it back together? Could Franklin
do it? Americans were desperate to find out.

Just as George Washington and Abraham Lincoln never gave up trying to save their country, fifty-one-year-old President Franklin D. "Doctor New Deal" Roosevelt was prepared to try anything to nurse his America back to health. On the day of his inauguration, March 4, 1933, he said to a crowd of hopeful citizens that "this great Nation will endure as it has endured, will revive, and will prosper." He told them that "the only thing we have to fear is fear itself."

Things happened fast. On March 9, President Roosevelt called for all the senators and representatives to meet in a special session of Congress. New laws would be needed to fix the national emergency. Three days later, he leaned into a microphone and talked to Americans as if all 125 million of them were sitting there with him. Franklin's clear plans and confident voice streamed out of a multitude of glowing radios. In this first of a series of "fireside chats," he explained to Americans what he was doing and why.

Plenty of banks had gone bust when too many folks tried to get their money out. So that the citizens would have faith in their banks, Franklin had closed every one. As bankers got their books in order, their doors would be reopened, and the people's savings would be guaranteed by the U.S. Treasury.

The lawmakers created programs that would get the country moving. Agencies such as the Civilian Conservation Corps (CCC) employed young men in conservation projects.

Road builders, carpenters, even writers and artists found work with the Works Progress Administration (WPA). The NRA (National Recovery Administration) made sure that businesses would be run fairly. There were so many agencies, all known by their initials, that folks joked about FDR's "alphabet soup." So many laws were passed in the first months of his presidency that this Hundred Days became famous in the history of the government of the United States.

Surrounded by papers and reports, his advisers, his secretary, reporters, his model ships, and a constant cloud of his own cigarette smoke, Franklin managed his difficult new job. He liked it. His lighthearted ways charmed people and helped them all to carry their heavy responsibilities. Eleanor had a new job, too, which she did not like at all. So she changed it.

The First Lady was expected to stick around the house and give parties. She and the President did entertain many a guest, but by 1936, when Franklin was reelected, Eleanor had traveled nearly 40,000 miles—by train, often by plane, sometimes driving in her own car. A chauffeur? No, thanks. She went wherever poor people suffered and struggled to get by. When she came home, she told Franklin how the New Deal was and wasn't working.

No First Lady had ever given a press conference. Eleanor, a confident speaker by now, regularly talked to female reporters about her busy doings and what ought to be done for the country. And it wasn't long before thousands of Americans were reading "My Day," Eleanor's daily newspaper column about her travels and ideas, her friends and family.

The First Lady was not supposed to get people stirred up. Eleanor did that often, especially when she tried to make life fairer for African-Americans. When a great performer was turned away from a concert hall because of the color of her skin, Eleanor found her a better place to sing. On Easter Sunday, 1939, on the steps of the Lincoln Memorial, Marian Anderson lifted her voice to a sea of joyful faces, light and dark, all hoping for better times ahead.

In the world of the 1930s, leaders arose out of people's longing for a better life. They promised the people of Russia, Italy, Spain, Germany, and Japan that they would lead them out of poverty to greatness. The Nazi government in Germany began persecuting the ones who, according to Adolf Hitler, were really the cause of all of Europe's sorrows: the Communists and the Jews. It wasn't long before Hitler was getting rid of those whom he did not want and grabbing what he did want: power for himself and land for a new German empire that would last a thousand years. "Conquest," he said, "is not only a right, but a duty."

War, it turned out, had only stopped to catch its breath in 1918. The forces of Japan advanced East and West in 1937 and 1938, and as German tanks rumbled into Poland in 1939, world war, greater and more terrible, began again. The new prime minister of England, Winston Churchill, was determined to save the free world. But could he do it without the American people? No. Did Americans want to fight in another war overseas? No! But when war came to them—in the form of Japan's attack on Pearl Harbor, Hawaii, on December 7, 1941—there was no longer any choice.

A pale, shaken Franklin Roosevelt, still sorrowing for his mother, Sara, who had died in September, told the Congress that "the American people in their righteous might will win through to absolute victory."

Lest bright windows attract the attention of enemy bombers, blackout curtains covered the windows of the White House. Behind them, lights burned late night after night as Franklin, Winston Churchill, and their military advisers planned how the Allies (fifty nations by 1945) would defeat the nine Axis powers, which included very powerful Germany and Japan.

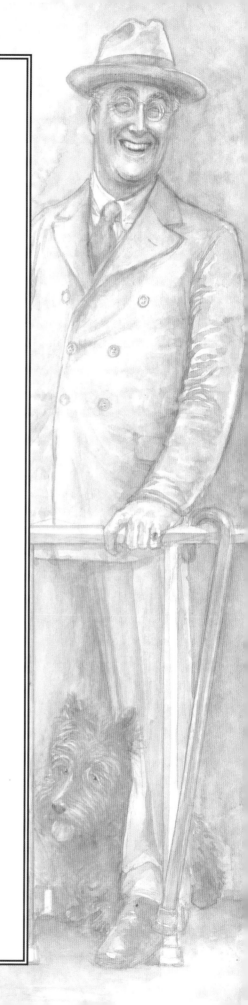

Through all the hard, slow Depression years, Franklin had encouraged the American people. He was tired, but now, in his third term as president, it was his job to get them ready for war— fast! More than twelve million men and women swelled the United States' armed forces. Franklin asked folks to volunteer at the Red Cross, plant gardens, gather metal and rubber, cut way back on gas and food, and buy bonds that would help pay for all-out war. Eleanor campaigned for fair treatment of African-Americans in the military and for day care for the thousands of children whose mothers were helping to build multitudes of tanks, warships, and bombers. The President's and First Lady's faces, their voices—even Franklin's Scottie, Fala— were familiar parts of the black-and-white newsreels at the movies in these pre-television times, these frightening, dangerous times.

Franklin traveled across the country and overseas to visit the troops and meet again with Winston Churchill and with their powerful ally, Joseph Stalin, the murderous premier of Russia. It was Eleanor, though, who donned a Red Cross uniform and weathered many a flight over the Atlantic, the South Pacific, and the Caribbean oceans to bring her husband's "deepest admiration" to thousands of wounded, homesick soldiers and sailors. The hard work each was doing gave the Roosevelts little time to worry over their four sons in uniform.

In spite of his weariness and a growing weakness in his heart, President Roosevelt was reelected in 1944. Perhaps at last, in Franklin's fourth term, the war would be won. The Allies had invaded Europe in June and begun the deadly eastward campaign to the heart of Germany. The terrible island-by-island battles against the Japanese in the South Pacific were still grinding on, but a secret weapon, an atomic bomb, was being developed that might end the gruesome war once and for all. Franklin devoutly hoped so. So many had died. He was so tired.

In the spring of 1945, Franklin and Eleanor planned to go to San Francisco, to the very first session of the United Nations (UN), an organization designed to keep the world at peace. Just before that trip, sixty-three-year-old Franklin decided to go to his house at Warm Springs, Georgia, for a little rest. He had always felt better there.

Less than two weeks later, on the evening of April 12, 1945, Eleanor sent for Vice President Truman. He hurried to the White House. The First Lady held her head high as she told him what had happened, then she hurried off to Georgia. Franklin had died of a stroke.

Eleanor brought her husband back to Washington. All along the way, crying people watched their train go by. Plenty of children had never known an America without smiling Franklin D. Roosevelt. It was left to President Harry S. Truman to oversee the terrible, joyous end of World War II.

UNITED STATES

Elliott Roosevelt's "Little Nell" became a great lady indeed in a world he never could have imagined. From the end of 1945 until 1952, Eleanor represented her nation at the UN. Here she accomplished her greatest work when she clearly spelled out how all of the world's people were entitled to be treated. Then she worked hard to get the nations of the war-wrecked world to agree to abide by the words she helped to draft in the Universal Declaration of Human Rights. The General Assembly of the UN approved it on December 10, 1948.

Until almost the end of her life, Eleanor wrote books full of memories, advice, and political observations. She spoke on radio and television. She worked for justice for less fortunate citizens and worked to gain votes for Democrats. In 1961, President John F. Kennedy asked her to return to the UN and lead a study of how women's interests were being served (or not) by the federal government.

But even the admired First Lady of the World could be ill, could be old and tired. Eleanor Roosevelt was seventy-eight years old when she died on November 7, 1962. Eleanor was buried beside Franklin at Hyde Park, under the familiar soil of Springwood's rose garden, near the wide Hudson River.

The world of privilege into which Franklin and Eleanor were born did not protect them from tragedy. But, in their personal battles to overcome troubles, they developed a solid respect for each other as well as the strength and compassion they needed to help Americans get through their nation's toughest times. Because they devoted their complicated lives to service, Franklin and Eleanor Roosevelt will always stand tall in the story of their country.

CHRONOLOGY

January 30, 1882 • Franklin Delano Roosevelt is born, Hyde Park, NY.

October 11, 1884 • Anna Eleanor Roosevelt is born, New York, NY.

December 7, 1892 • Anna Eleanor Hall Roosevelt (ER's mother) dies.

August 14, 1894 • Elliott Roosevelt (ER's father) dies.

December 8, 1900 • James Roosevelt (FDR's father) dies.

March 17, 1905 • Franklin and Eleanor Roosevelt are married in New York City.

May 3, 1906 • Anna Eleanor, their daughter, is born.

December 23, 1907 • James is born.

March 18, 1909 • Franklin is born. He dies on November 8, 1909.

September 23, 1910 • Elliott is born.

August 17, 1914 • Franklin Delano, Jr., is born.

March 13, 1916 • John Aspinwall Roosevelt is born.

June 28, 1914 • Archduke Franz Ferdinand is assassinated in Sarajevo, Bosnia, touching off World War I.

April 6, 1917 • President Woodrow Wilson declares war on Germany. United States enters WWI.

November 11, 1918 • Armistice is declared. The fighting in World War I ends.

January 6, 1919 • Theodore Roosevelt dies.

August 10–11, 1921 • Franklin falls ill with polio at Campobello Island, Maine.

November 6, 1928 • FDR is elected governor of New York (reelected November 4,1930).

October 29, 1929 • The stock market crashes, ushering in the Great Depression.

November 8, 1932 • FDR is elected 32nd president. He will be reelected in 1936, 1940, and 1944, thus occupying the office of president longer than anyone in U.S. history.

September 1, 1939 • German forces invade Poland and World War II begins.

Christmas, 1940 • Fala, FDR's Scottie, comes to live in the White House.

September 7, 1941 • Sara Delano Roosevelt (FDR's mother) dies at Springwood, Hyde Park, NY.

December 7, 1941 • Empire of Japan attacks U.S. at Pearl Harbor, Hawaii.

April 12, 1945 • FDR dies in Warm Springs, GA. Harry S. Truman becomes the 33rd president.

April 30, 1945 • Adolf Hitler kills himself in his hideout in Berlin, Germany.

May 8, 1945 • Germany surrenders. V-E Day—Victory in Europe.

August 6, 1945 • Atomic bomb is dropped on Hiroshima, Japan.

September 2, 1945 • Japan surrenders. V-J Day—Victory in Japan.

December 31, 1945–December 31, 1952 • Eleanor Roosevelt is U.S. delegate at the United Nations.

February 16, 1946 • Eleanor becomes chairman of the UN's Human Rights Commission.

November 7, 1962 • Eleanor Roosevelt dies in New York City.

BIBLIOGRAPHY

Alsop, Joseph. *FDR: A Centenary Remembrance*. New York: Viking Press, 1982.

Collier, Peter, and David Horowitz. *The Roosevelts: An American Saga*. New York: Simon and Schuster, 1994.

Freeman, Russell. *Eleanor Roosevelt: A Life of Discovery*. New York: Clarion Books, 1993.

———*Franklin Delano Roosevelt*. New York: Clarion Books, 1990.

Goodwin, Doris Kearns. *No Ordinary Time*. New York: Simon and Schuster, 1994.

Taylor, Tim. *The Book of Presidents*. New York: Arno Press, 1972.

Contact Information for the homes of Franklin and Eleanor Roosevelt:

Home of Franklin D. Roosevelt National Historic Site, 4097 Albany Post Road, Hyde Park, New York 12538-1997 www.nps.gov/hofr. phone: 845-229-9115

Little White House State Historic Site, 401 Little White House Road, Georgia Highway 85 Alternate, Warm Springs, Georgia 31830. www.fdr~littlewhitehouse.org phone: 706-655-5870